# Rock Guitar Playing
# Grade Four

**Compiled by
Tony Skinner and Merv Young
on behalf of
Registry Of Guitar Tutors
www.RGT.org**

Printed and bound in Great Britain

A CIP record for this publication is available from the British Library
**ISBN: 978-1-905908-34-9**

Published by Registry Publications

Registry Mews, Wilton Rd, Bexhill, Sussex, TN40 1HY

Cover photo by Andreas Gradin/Fotolia.  Design by JAK Images.

Compiled by

**www.RGT.org**

v.20111101

# Contents

# Introduction

This book is part of a progressive series of ten handbooks designed for rock guitarists who wish to develop their playing and obtain a qualification. Although the primary intention of these handbooks is to prepare candidates for the Registry Of Guitar Tutors (RGT) rock guitar exams, the series also provides a comprehensive structure that will help develop the abilities of any guitarist interested in rock music, whether or not intending to take an exam.

Those preparing for an exam should use this handbook in conjunction with the *Syllabus for Rock Guitar Playing* and the *Rock Guitar Exam Information Booklet* – both freely downloadable from the RGT website: **www.RGT.org**

## Exam Outline

There are three components to this exam, each of which is briefly outlined below:

❶ **Prepared Performances.** The performance, along to backing tracks, of special arrangements of two classic rock pieces. Alternatively, one piece may be replaced by a 'free choice' piece.

❷ **Improvisation.** This is in two parts: firstly, improvisation of a lead guitar solo over a previously unseen chord progression, followed by improvisation of a rhythm guitar part over the same chord progression. Playing will be to a backing track provided by the examiner.

❸ **Aural Assessment.** This will consist of a 'Rhythm Test' (repeating the rhythm of a riff), a 'Pitch Test' (reproducing a riff on the guitar) and a 'Chord Recognition Test' (reproducing a short chord sequence).

## Mark Scheme

The maximum marks available for each component are:

- Prepared Performances: 60 marks (30 marks per piece).
- Improvisation: 30 marks.
- Aural Assessment: 10 marks.

To pass the exam candidates need a total of 65 marks. Candidates achieving 75 marks will be awarded a Merit certificate, or a Distinction certificate for 85 marks or above.

## Exam Entry

An exam entry form is provided at the rear of this handbook. This is the only valid entry form for the RGT rock guitar playing exams. Please note that if the entry form is detached and lost, it will not be replaced under any circumstances and the candidate will be required to obtain a replacement handbook to obtain another entry form. The entry form includes a unique entry code to enable online entry via the RGT website **www.RGT.org**

## Notation

Within this handbook, scales and chords are illustrated in three formats: traditional notation, tablature and fretboxes – thereby ensuring that there is no doubt as to how to play each scale or chord. Each of these methods of notation is explained below.

### Traditional Notation:

Each line, and space between lines, represents a different note. Leger lines are used to extend the stave for low or high notes. For scales, fret and string numbers are printed below the notation: fret-hand fingering is shown with the numbers 1 2 3 4, with 0 indicating an open string; string numbers are shown in a circle. The example above shows a two-octave C major scale.

### Tablature:

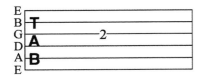

Horizontal lines represent the strings (with the top line being the high E string). The numbers on the string lines refer to the frets. 0 on a line means play that string open (unfretted). This example means play at the second fret on the third string.

### Fretboxes:

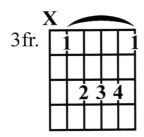

Vertical lines represent the strings – with the line furthest to the right representing the high E string. Horizontal lines represent the frets. The numbers on the lines show the recommended fingering. 1 represents the index finger, 2 = the long middle finger, 3 = the ring finger, 4 = the little finger. An X above a string line indicates that the string should not be played. Where a barré chord, or partial barré, needs to be played a curved line appears above the fretbox; the starting fret position is shown to the left of the fretbox. This example shows the fretbox for a C major barré chord at the third fret.

### Fingering Options

The fret-hand fingerings that have been chosen are those that are most likely to be effective for the widest range of players at this level. However, there are a variety of alternative fingerings that could be used, and any systematic and effective fingerings that produce a good musical result will be acceptable; there is no requirement to use the exact fingerings shown within this handbook.

### Tuning

For exam purposes guitars should be tuned to Standard Concert Pitch (A=440Hz). The use of an electronic tuner or other tuning aid is permitted. The examiner will not assist with tuning other than to, upon request, offer an E or A note to tune to.

# Prepared Performances

Candidates should choose and perform TWO of the following classic rock pieces:

❶ *Layla* – Derek and the Dominos

❷ *All Along the Watchtower* – The Jimi Hendrix Experience

❸ *Sweet Home Alabama* – Lynyrd Skynyrd

❹ *Walk This Way* – Aerosmith

If preferred, candidates can substitute a 'free choice' piece for one of the listed pieces, provided it is of at least a similar standard and does not exceed five minutes duration. (See more information about the requirements for a free choice piece at the end of this chapter.)

## Obtaining the notation and audio

The pieces listed above have been specifically arranged for the RGT Grade Four Rock Guitar Playing exam and are notated in TAB and standard notation in the publication *Graded Rock Guitar Songs – 8 Rock Classics for Intermediate Guitarists\**. This also includes a CD that features each track being performed in full, as well as a backing track for each piece for the candidate to perform with. On the recordings, the vocal melody line has been played fairly low in the mix on guitar; the purpose of including the melody line is simply to provide a guide during the performance as to where in the song you are.

\* For copyright ownership reasons, the notation and audio tracks for the listed classic rock pieces cannot be included in this RGT grade handbook. However, they are all included in the book *Graded Rock Guitar Songs – 8 Rock Classics for Intermediate Guitarists* which is available from <u>www.BooksForGuitar.com</u> or can be ordered from most music stores. The book also contains all the performance pieces that are required for the RGT rock guitar playing Grade Five exam.

## Exam format

Candidates' performances should be accurate reproductions of the specially arranged versions of the pieces as notated and recorded in the book *Graded Rock Guitar Songs – 8 Rock Classics for Intermediate Guitarists*. Alternative fingerings and playing positions can be adopted if preferred, provided the overall musical result is not altered from the recorded version.

The performances should be played along to the specially recorded backing tracks supplied on the CD that is included with the book *Graded Rock Guitar Songs – 8 Rock Classics for Intermediate Guitarists.* Alternative recordings of the pieces will not be accepted as backing tracks. There is no need to bring the CD from this book to the exam, as the examiner will have these backing tracks.

Prior to the performance commencing, candidates will be allowed a brief 'soundcheck' so that they can choose their sound and volume level. Candidates can use either a clean or a distorted guitar sound for their performance of these tracks, and can bring their own distortion or other effects units to the exam *providing that* they can set them up promptly and unaided.

In order to achieve the maximum mark in this section of the exam, performances should be fully accurate and very confidently presented. Timing, clarity and technical control should be totally secure throughout and some expressive qualities should be displayed. Candidates are encouraged to perform the pieces from memory, although this is *not* a requirement.


## Performance Tips


### *Layla* – Derek and the Dominos

There are several different guitar parts on the original artist's version of this track, so follow the notation carefully throughout to ensure that your performance is accurate to the exam arrangement. The opening 16th note lick is played using hammer-ons and pull-offs and these need to be played smoothly and fluently to ensure that the rhythm is accurate and even. This lick is then played two octaves higher, starting at fret 10 on the B string. Listen to the recorded track carefully here to ensure the longer notes that follow the initial lick are all allowed to ring out for their full value.

The chords that feature in the verse are performed using a variety of different techniques. The first C#m chord should sound for its full length, whereas the remaining three C#m chords in the same bar should be cut short to produce a clipped 'staccato' sound. The damped F#m7 chord can be performed by resting the fingers of the fretting hand gently against the strings whilst strumming, although this effect may occur naturally as you release the pressure of the fretting fingers to change to the next chord. The large fretboard movement from the open E chord at the end of the verse up to fret 10 to commence the chorus lick may take a little practice to perfect.

The chorus features a return of the main licks that appeared in the introduction and is repeated several times. Maintaining the accuracy of the rhythm and the string bends whilst repeating these licks may take some practice, so prepare slowly and carefully here to build up the stamina in your finger muscles.

### *All Along The Watchtower* – The Jimi Hendrix Experience

The introduction starts with a chordal riff before switching to a short lead guitar solo. String bends dominate this solo, so care needs to be taken to ensure that the pitch of the string bends is accurate.

The verse features a simplified version of the chord-based fills that occur in the original version of the song. The fills are played using a combination of a hammer-on and pull-off and will need to be executed fluently and smoothly so that the rhythm of the chord sequence is not interrupted. The instrumental section that follows features the same chords as the verse but with a busier rhythm pattern. Take care to ensure that the damped 16$^{th}$ note chords are played fluently.

The final verses use the same chord progression again, but with a variation on the playing style. The guitar solo in the outro includes a series of repeated, unison string bends that move up the guitar neck. The biggest challenge here is to ensure that the pitch of each string bend matches the pitch of the fretted note on the top E string.

### *Sweet Home Alabama* – Lynyrd Skynyrd

Listen carefully to the demonstration track to help capture the distinctive rhythm that is used in the introduction. The fills that occur after the G major chords in the introduction are tricky to execute at first, so practise these separately first to ensure that the notes are played smoothly and fluently.

The chords in the verse have a clipped feel on the bass notes; bring your picking hand gently against the strings to cut the notes on the open strings short, or release the pressure slightly with your fretting hand if the note is not an open string.

The instrumental section that follows the verse contains a number of slides and hammer-ons that lend fluidity to the phrases but may require some careful practice to execute smoothly. Try to ensure that the rhythm of the notes is being played correctly when employing these techniques, and listen to the recorded track carefully to ensure that you are familiar with how this section should sound.

The chorus incorporates a series of short riffs that enhance the accompaniment chords, these are interspersed midway by a repetitive 16$^{th}$ note phrase that uses flowing hammer-ons. Listen to and practise this section carefully, as accurate performance of the rhythm here can be a challenge.

### *Walk This Way* – Aerosmith

The introduction riff features 16$^{th}$ notes and may require some practice to play at the required tempo. Take care to observe the rests that occur in this introduction; bring your picking hand against the strings to silence them cleanly.

The verse riff contains a C5 power chord followed by a four-note phrase that draws on the rhythmic feel of the original Aerosmith recording. There are a number of fingering options available here as you switch from the power chord to the four-note phrase, so try to adopt a fingering approach that allows this change to be performed fluently. When the introduction riff returns in the latter part of the verse make sure to damp the notes on the low E string where marked, by resting your fretting hand against the string whilst picking the notated rhythm. Also, notice the subtle variation in timing between the riff in the introduction and how it is played in the verse.

The chorus includes a repeated double-note lick with a slight string bend on the B string at fret 4. Take care here to ensure that only the B string is slightly bent up, try not to bend the 5th fret note on the top E string as well.

The coda incorporates a variation on the introduction riff, switching between starting on the low E and A strings. Practise this slowly at first and build up the speed and stamina gradually.

## Free Choice Piece

If the candidate opts to perform a piece of their own choosing in place of one of the listed pieces, then this free choice piece should be performed over a backing track that is supplied (but not necessarily recorded) by the candidate. The backing track must be in CD format, as exam venues will normally only be equipped for CD playback.

The free choice piece should be rock-orientated in both performance style and arrangement.

Where the piece originally contains an improvised guitar solo, candidates can either reproduce this or alternatively can perform their own solo – providing this includes an appropriate level of technical content for the grade.

The free choice piece can be the candidate's own composition, but this is not a requirement and the compositional element of any piece will not be assessed.

The use of altered tuning for the free choice piece is allowable, providing that the candidate is able to re-tune their guitar promptly and unaided or, if preferred, the candidate may bring to the exam an additional pre-tuned guitar.

If the technical standard of the free choice piece is significantly below that of those listed for the grade, this may be reflected in the mark awarded.

# Improvisation

The candidate will be shown a previously unseen chord chart in $\frac{4}{4}$ time. This will consist of an 8-bar chord progression, which will be played five times non-stop (via a pre-recorded backing track).

- During the first verse, the candidate should just listen to the track while reading the chord chart.

- A 4-beat count-in will be given and then during the next two verses, the candidate should improvise a lead guitar solo.

- A 4-beat count-in will be given and then during the last two verses, the candidate should improvise a rhythm guitar part.

- The backing track will end with the first chord of the progression played once.

Candidates will be given a short time to study the chord chart and will then be allowed a brief 'soundcheck' with the track prior to the performance commencing, so that they can choose their sound and volume level. Candidates can bring their own distortion or other effects units to the exam *providing that* they can set them up promptly and unaided.

The backing track will include drums, bass and rhythm guitar for the first three verses, but in the last two verses the recorded rhythm guitar part will be omitted so that the candidate can perform their own rhythm guitar part.

The rhythm guitar part that is recorded on the backing track gives an indication of the standard of rhythm playing that is expected for this section of the exam. Candidates do not need to reproduce exactly the rhythm part that is recorded on the backing track. They should, however, strive to perform a rhythm part that is stylistically appropriate and with a "feel" that is in keeping with the backing track. Part of the assessment here will be centred on the candidate's ability to listen and then perform an appropriate rhythm part.

The range of chords that may appear in the backing tracks for this grade is detailed overleaf. As the chord progression will be previously unseen by the candidate, the candidate will need to be fully familiar with all the chords listed for the grade in order to be properly prepared for the chord progressions that will occur in the exam. Each chord progression will consist of chords grouped together into appropriate keys. Several examples of the type of chord progression that will occur at this grade are provided at the end of this chapter.

# Chords

Here is the range of chords that may occur in the chord progressions for this grade.

| | | |
|---|---|---|
| • | **Major barré chords:** | **at any pitch** |
| • | **Minor barré chords:** | **at any pitch** |
| • | **Fifth (power) chords:** | **at any pitch** |

The barré and fifth chords below are illustrated with a root note of C, however, these chord shapes are all 'transpositional' – i.e. they can be moved up or down the fretboard to any pitch without the need to change fingering.

In order to avoid large fingerboard shifts, two shapes are provided for each chord type: one with its root note on the E string and one with its root note on the A string. When playing the chord progressions, candidates should carefully select which position to play each chord in – so as to avoid large cumbersome shifts up or down the fretboard.

This table lists the first finger fret position needed to produce chords at different pitches.

| Barré on fret: | 1 | 2 | 3 | 4 | 5 | 6 | 7 | 8 | 9 | 10 | 11 | 12 |
|---|---|---|---|---|---|---|---|---|---|---|---|---|
| Root on E string: | F | F#/Gb | G | G#/Ab | A | A#/Bb | B | C | C#/Db | D | D#/Eb | E |
| Root on A string: | A#/Bb | B | C | C#/Db | D | D#/Eb | E | F | F#/Gb | G | G#/Ab | A |

### C major – root on E string

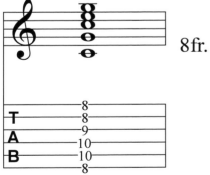 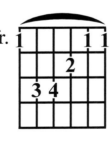

### C major – root on A string

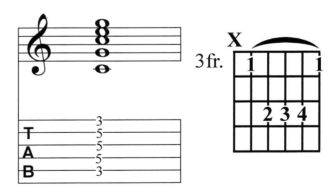

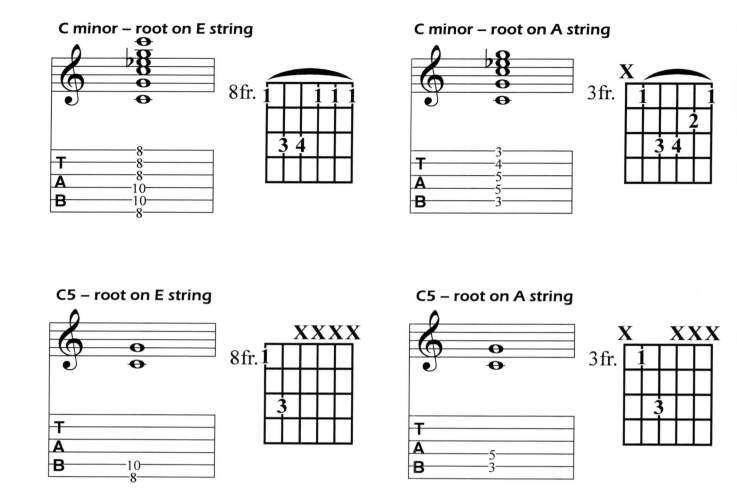

**C minor – root on E string**

**C minor – root on A string**

**C5 – root on E string**

**C5 – root on A string**

## Barré Chord Playing Advice

In barré chords the first finger effectively replaces the nut and acts as a 'bar' across all the strings.  In chords with the root note on the A string, although you can still place the first finger barré over all six strings, you should omit the sixth string in your strum (as indicated by the symbol 'X' in the fretboxes above).

To ensure that your barré chords ring clearly you should observe the following advice:

◊　　The first finger should be straight and in-line with the fret, rather than at an angle to it.

◊　　The first finger need not be completely flat: it can be tilted very slightly away from the fret toward its outer side.

◊　　Position the first finger so that the creases at its joints do not coincide with the strings; if necessary, adjust the barré until you find the optimum position.

◊　　Ensure that fretting fingers, other than the first finger, remain upright and press against the strings with their tips.

◊　　Do not exert excessive pressure with either the first finger or the thumb.

◊　　All fingers should be positioned as close to the fretwire as possible.

# Scales

In order to improvise a lead guitar solo accurately and effectively, candidates will need to learn a range of appropriate scales upon which to base their improvisation. In the exam, the first chord in the progression will be the key chord and will, therefore, indicate the scale that would generally be best to use for improvising a lead solo; a recommended scale that could be used to improvise over each progression type is listed below. Although other scale options and improvisation approaches exist, it is highly recommended that candidates acquire a thorough knowledge of the scales listed for the grade, as these will provide a core foundation for improvisation at the appropriate level of technical development. However, providing they produce an effective musical result, other appropriate scale choices or improvisation approaches will also be acceptable.

The examiner will not provide any advice regarding identifying the key or guidance on which scale to use. However, *for the purposes of this exam grade*, candidates can bear in mind the following:

- If the starting chord is minor, then a natural minor or pentatonic minor scale (with the same starting pitch) could be used.
- If the starting chord is major, then a major or pentatonic major scale (with the same starting pitch) could be used.
- If the progression starts with a fifth chord, then a blues scale or pentatonic minor scale (with the same starting pitch) could be used.

Here is the range of scales recommended for use during the lead guitar improvisation section of the exam at this grade.

| | |
|---|---|
| • Natural minor scale: | in any key |
| • Pentatonic minor scale: | in any key |
| • Blues scale: | in any key |
| • Major scale: | in any key |
| • Pentatonic major scale: | in any key |

Improvisation using two-octave fretted scales is expected at this grade.

The scales overleaf are all illustrated with a key note of C, however, these scale shapes are all 'transpositional' – i.e. they can be moved up or down the fretboard to any key without the need to change fingering.

This table lists the fret on the E (6<sup>th</sup>) string that can be used to start each scale, depending upon the key required.

| Starting fret: | 1/13 | 2/14 | 3/15 | 4 | 5 | 6 | 7 | 8 | 9 | 10 | 11 | 12 |
|---|---|---|---|---|---|---|---|---|---|---|---|---|
| Keynote: | F | F#/Gb | G | G#/Ab | A | A#/Bb | B | C | C#/Db | D | D#/Eb | E |

### C natural minor scale – 2 octaves
C D Eb F G Ab Bb C

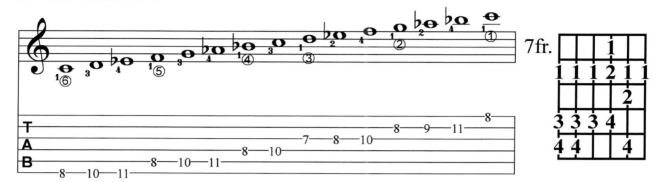

### C pentatonic minor scale – 2 octaves
C Eb F G Bb C

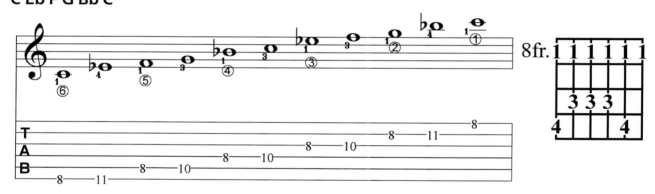

### C blues scale – 2 octaves
C Eb F Gb G Bb C

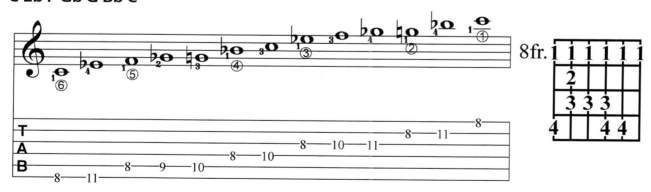

## C major scale – 2 octaves
C D E F G A B C

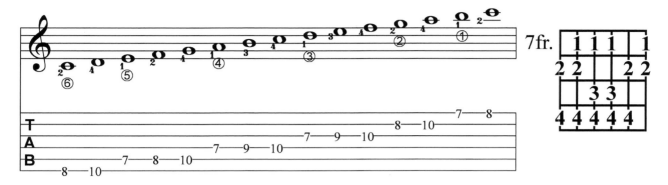

7fr.

## C pentatonic major scale – 2 octaves
C D E G A C

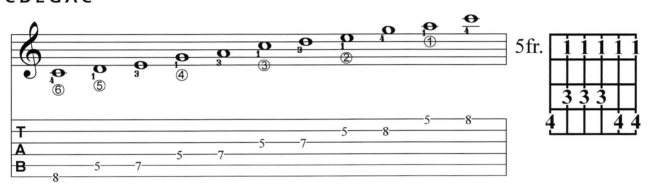

5fr.

## Performance Advice

In order to attain maximum marks in this section of the exam, the performance needs to be fully accurate and confident in execution, with a high level of clarity and fluency appropriate to the grade. There should be evidence of stylistic interpretation, inventiveness and creativity.

As the improvised rhythm playing will be performed over a recorded backing track, the emphasis will be on developing key performance skills such as rhythmic security and fluency. Dynamic markings are not included on the chord charts, to enable candidates to focus on their own dynamic interpretation. Candidates should be able to control any volume changes that are needed when switching from lead to rhythm playing. Candidates are encouraged to incorporate the use of rhythm guitar techniques such as palm-muting, 'ghost-strums', staccato etc. into their playing, where this would appropriately enhance the musical performance.

The improvised lead solo should be accurate in terms of note selection and timing in relation to the accompaniment. There should be evidence of melodic phrasing and shaping. The use of specialist techniques such as string bending, vibrato, slides and slurs (i.e. hammer-ons and pull-offs) should be used to enhance the musical performance, and some use of these techniques is expected to be demonstrated at this grade, when musically appropriate.

# Performance Tips

➢ Try to use the short period of study time, when you're first shown the chord chart, as effectively as possible by looking through the chart to ensure you are confident with the chords that occur and with your choice of scale.

➢ During the first verse of the backing track, follow the chord chart carefully and get ready to start your lead guitar improvisation after the 4 beat count-in.

➢ Listen carefully to the backing track throughout the performance to ensure that your lead and rhythm playing is rhythmically secure; try to make your playing relate to what the bass and drums are playing.

➢ Keep an awareness of where you are in the chord chart, so that the 4 beat count-in to commence your rhythm playing doesn't take you by surprise – as the examiner will not re-start the backing track once it is underway.

➢ When switching to rhythm playing, you will almost certainly need to quickly adjust the volume on your guitar, as the settings you have used for lead playing may overpower the accompaniment if used for rhythm playing.

➢ During the lead improvising listen carefully to what you are playing to make it sound as musically effective as you can and try to create musical phrases. Use techniques such as string bends, vibrato and slurs to enhance the expressiveness of your lead solo.

➢ Prior to exam day, when preparing for this section of the exam ensure that you are completely confident knowing, and changing between, all the chords that may occur; during the exam itself you can then focus on playing the chords as confidently and musically as possible.

➢ The example chord charts that are provided overleaf give an indication of what to expect in the exam, but these are not the actual charts that will be presented in the exam. In preparing for this section of the exam you are advised to download all these example backing tracks to ensure that you are comfortable with improvising both lead and rhythm parts over the range of tempos and styles indicated by these examples. Recordings of all the example chord charts included in this handbook can be downloaded from **www.DownloadsForGuitar.com**

## Example Chord Progressions

The following are examples of the type of chord progression candidates may be presented with in this section of the exam. Note that the scale suggestions shown above each progression will NOT appear in the charts presented during the exam.

### Improvisation Chart Example 1

C pentatonic minor scale could be used to improvise over this progression.

| $\frac{4}{4}$ Cm | Fm | B♭ | Gm | |
|---|---|---|---|---|
| Cm | A♭ | B♭ | B♭ | ‖ |

### Improvisation Chart Example 2

F# natural minor scale could be used to improvise over this progression.

| $\frac{4}{4}$ F♯m | E | F♯m | Bm | |
|---|---|---|---|---|
| F♯m | D | Bm | C♯m | ‖ |

### Improvisation Chart Example 3

Ab major scale could be used to improvise over this progression.

| $\frac{4}{4}$ A♭ | E♭ | Fm | D♭ | |
|---|---|---|---|---|
| A♭ | B♭m | D♭ | E♭ | ‖ |

## Improvisation Chart Example 4

Bb pentatonic major scale could be used to improvise over this progression.

| $\frac{4}{4}$ Bb | | Cm | | Dm | | Cm | |
| --- | --- | --- | --- | --- | --- | --- | --- |
| Gm | | Dm | | Cm | | F | ‖ |

## Improvisation Chart Example 5

C blues scale could be used to improvise over this progression.

| $\frac{4}{4}$ C5 | | C5 | | Bb5 | | F5 | |
| --- | --- | --- | --- | --- | --- | --- | --- |
| C5 | | Eb5 | | F5 | | G5 | ‖ |

It is important to note that the sample chord progressions provided above are supplied purely to provide examples of the *type* of chord progression that may occur in the exam. These examples are NOT the actual chord progressions that candidates will be given in the exam.

---

### Listen and Practise

Audio recordings of all the above examples, with backing tracks in the style of those that will be used in the exam, can be downloaded from
www.DownloadsForGuitar.com

# Aural Assessment

Candidates' aural abilities will be assessed via a series of three aural tests:

• Rhythm test

• Pitch test

• Chord recognition test

## Rhythm Test

A riff is played three times via a recording. During the third playing the candidate is required to clap along with the exact *rhythm* of the riff.

At this grade, the riff will be two bars in length. The time signature will be $^4_4$. Note durations will not be shorter than 16th notes (semiquavers).

Examples of the *type* of riffs that will occur at this grade are shown overleaf, with the rhythm to be clapped notated below the tab.

## Pitch Test

The riff from the rhythm test is played two further times with a click track. A gap is left after each playing, so that the candidate can practise the riff. Then, after a one-bar count-in, the candidate is required to play along with a click track, accurately reproducing the riff on the guitar.

At this grade, the range of scales from which the riff will be derived is limited to those listed in the improvisation section of this handbook, i.e. natural minor, pentatonic minor, major, pentatonic major or blues scale. The riff will start on the keynote and may be in *any* key. The examiner will state which scale the riff is taken from.

Overleaf are some examples of the *type* of riffs that will occur at this grade in the rhythm and pitch tests.

### Example 1 (from A blues scale)

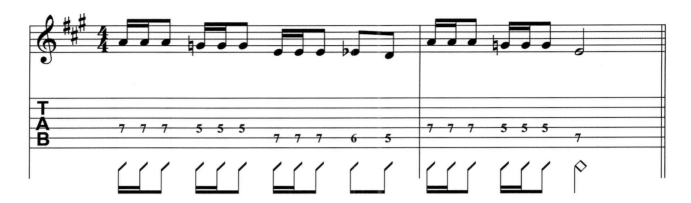

### Example 2 (from F natural minor scale)

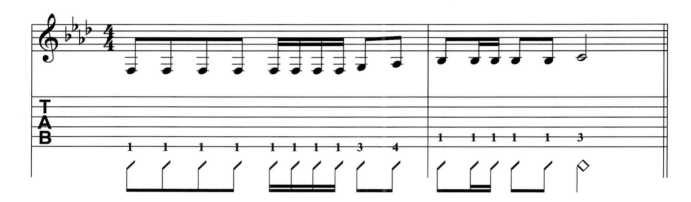

### Example 3 (from A major scale)

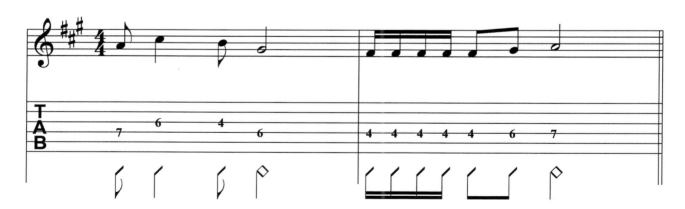

**Example 4 (from C pentatonic minor scale)**

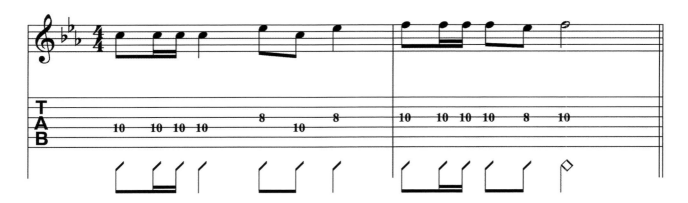

**Example 5 (from C pentatonic major scale)**

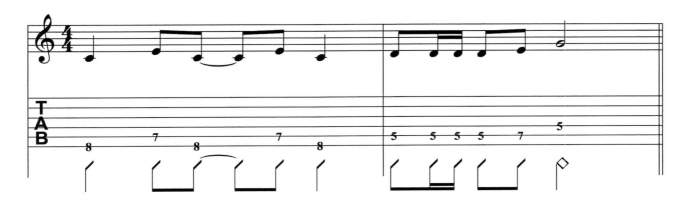

# Chord Recognition Test

A four-bar chord progression will be played four times, using a simple strumming rhythm. During the fourth playing, candidates should play along accurately reproducing the chords. Candidates can practise playing along during previous playings, but will only be assessed during the fourth playing.

The chord progression will consist of the following chords: G5 C5 D5 E5. There will be one bar of each chord. The progression will start on G5; the other chords may follow in any order.

The progression will be played using fretted 5th (power) chords, but candidates do not need to play the chords in the same positions as on the recording, nor do they need to copy the exact rhythm of the strumming provided the overall timing is secure; the assessment will focus on the accurate reproduction of the chord pitches.

Below are some examples of the *type* of chord progressions that will occur at this grade in the chord recognition tests.

**Example 1**

| $\frac{4}{4}$ G5 | C5 | D5 | E5 ||

**Example 2**

| $\frac{4}{4}$ G5 | D5 | C5 | E5 ||

**Example 3**

| $\frac{4}{4}$ G5 | E5 | C5 | D5 ||

**Example 4**

| $\frac{4}{4}$ G5 | E5 | D5 | C5 ||

**Example 5**

| $\frac{4}{4}$ G5 | C5 | E5 | D5 ||

**Example 6**

| $\frac{4}{4}$ G5 | D5 | E5 | C5 ||

---

**Listen and Practise**

Audio recordings of all the aural tests in this handbook can be downloaded from
www.DownloadsForGuitar.com

---

# Exam Entry Form
# Rock Guitar Grade ④

## ONLINE ENTRY – AVAILABLE FOR UK CANDIDATES ONLY

For **UK candidates**, entries and payments can be made online at www.RGT.org, using the entry code below. You will be able to pay the entry fee by credit or debit card at a secure payment page on the website.

Your unique and confidential exam entry code is:

### RD-5931-AD

*Keep this unique code confidential, as it can only be used once.* Once you have entered online, you should sign this form overleaf. **You must bring this signed form to your exam and hand it to the examiner in order to be admitted to the exam room.**

---

*If NOT entering online, please complete BOTH sides of this form and return to the address overleaf.*

SESSION (Spring/Summer/Winter): _____ YEAR: _____

Dates/times NOT available: _____

Note: Only name *specific* dates (and times on those dates) when it would be *absolutely impossible* for you to attend due to important prior commitments (such as pre-booked overseas travel) which cannot be cancelled. We will then endeavour to avoid scheduling an exam session in your area on those dates. In fairness to all other candidates in your area, **only list dates on which it would be impossible for you to attend**. An entry form that blocks out unreasonable periods may be returned. (Exams may be held on any day of the week including, but not exclusively, weekends. Exams may be held within or outside of the school term.)

### *Candidate Details:* *Please write as clearly as possible using BLOCK CAPITALS*

Candidate Name (as to appear on certificate): _____

Address: _____

_____ Postcode: _____

Tel. No. (day): _____ (mobile): _____

**IMPORTANT: Take care to write your email address below as clearly as possible, as your exam entry acknowledgement and your exam appointment details will be sent to this email address. Only provide an email address that is in regular monitored use.**

Email:_____
**Where an email address is provided your exam correspondence will be sent by email only, and not by post. This will ensure your exam correspondence will reach you sooner.**

### *Teacher Details* (if applicable)

Teacher Name (as to appear on certificate): _____

RGT Tutor Code (if applicable):_____

Address: _____

_____ Postcode: _____

Tel. No. (day): _____ (mobile): _____

Email:_____

# RGT Rock Guitar Official Entry Form

**The standard LCM entry form is NOT valid for RGT exam entries.**
**Entry to the exam is only possible via this original form.**
**Photocopies of this form will not be accepted under any circumstances.**

- Completion of this entry form is an agreement to comply with the current syllabus requirements and conditions of entry published at www.RGT.org. Where candidates are entered for exams by a teacher, parent or guardian that person hereby takes responsibility that the candidate is entered in accordance with the current syllabus requirements and conditions of entry.

- If you are being taught by an *RGT registered* tutor, please hand this completed form to your tutor and request him/her to administer the entry on your behalf.

- For candidates with special needs, a letter giving details should be attached.

Exam Fee: £_____     Late Entry Fee (if applicable): £_____

Total amount submitted: £_____

Cheques or postal orders should be made payable to Registry of Guitar Tutors.

Details of conditions of entry, entry deadlines and exam fees are obtainable from the RGT website: www.RGT.org

Once an entry has been accepted, entry fees cannot be refunded.

## CANDIDATE INFORMATION (UK Candidates only)

In order to meet our obligations in monitoring the implementation of equal opportunities policies, UK candidates are required to supply the information requested below. The information provided will in no way whatsoever influence the marks awarded during the exam.

Date of birth: _____ Age: _____ Gender – please circle: male / female

Ethnicity (please enter 2 digit code from chart below): _____ Signed: _____

**ETHNIC ORIGIN CLASSIFICATIONS** (If you prefer not to say, write '17' in the space above.)

White: **01 British**     **02 Irish**     **03 Other white background**

Mixed: **04 White & black Caribbean**     **05 White & black African**     **06 White & Asian**     **07 Other mixed background**

Asian or Asian British: **08 Indian**     **09 Pakistani**     **10 Bangladeshi**     **11 Other Asian background**

Black or Black British: **12 Caribbean**     **13 African**     **14 Other black background**

Chinese or Other Ethnic Group: **15 Chinese**     **16 Other**     **17 Prefer not to say**

I understand and accept the current syllabus regulations and conditions of entry for this exam as specified on the RGT website.

Signed by candidate (if aged 18 or over) _____ Date _____

If candidate is under 18, this form should be signed by a parent/guardian/teacher (circle which applies):

Signed _____ Name_____ Date_____

## UK ENTRIES

See overleaf for details of how to enter online OR return this form to:
**Registry of Guitar Tutors, Registry Mews, 11 to 13 Wilton Road, Bexhill-on-Sea, E. Sussex, TN40 1HY**
(If you have submitted your entry online do NOT post this form, instead you need to sign it above and hand it to the examiner on the day of your exam.)
To contact the RGT office telephone 01424 222222 or Email office@RGT.org

## NON-UK ENTRIES

To locate the address within your country that entry forms should be sent to, and to view exam fees in your currency, visit the RGT website **www.RGT.org** and navigate to the 'RGT Worldwide' section.